Godot Imagine Godot

Books by Nathaniel Hutner

Heracleitus Under Water 1988

War: A Book Of Poems 2003

The Name We Never Lose 2019

The Complete Poems of Nathaniel Hutner 2021

☙

Plays by Nathaniel Hutner

Godot Arrives

Godot Imagine Godot

Godot at Night

Godot, Alive or Dead

The President Pardons Godot

☙

Short Plays by Nathaniel Hutner

Hot Potatoes

The Fix

Keewaydin Plays

Godot Imagine Godot

※

A Comedy by Nathaniel Hutner

Burlington, Vermont

A collected edition of Nathaniel Hutner's plays, ***The Collected Plays of Nathaniel Hutner***, is available from Onion River Press, 191 Bank Street, Burlington, VT 05401

Copyright © 2021 by Nathaniel Hutner

All rights reserved. No part of this publication may be reproduced, distributed, or transmitted in any form or by any means, including photocopying, recording, or other electronic or mechanical methods, without the prior written permission of the publisher, except in the case of brief quotations embodied in critical reviews and certain other noncommercial uses permitted by copyright law.

Onion River Press
191 Bank Street
Burlington, VT 05401

ISBN: 978-1-949066-90-6

Library of Congress Control Number: 2021914319

Designed by Jenny Lyons, Middlebury VT

Godot Imagine Godot

INMATES

GODOT

DANIEL: Son of A and B

A: Visiting from the Outer Hebrides

MR. MALAPROP: B in disguise

UNCLE STURTEVANT: A Southerner suffering from megalomania

LADY DALY: A large black woman in her early thirties, manic-depressive with aggressive tendencies

DOTTIE DUMPLING: A maid, thin

LUCILLE OUTBACK: A Society Person

ALICE, PRINCESS OF LIVERMORE: An Oxford undergraduate

DR. LANCELOT HABIT: Resident-in-Chief

ACT I

SCENE 1

The action (or inaction) takes place at the Budinger Foundation, a psychiatric hospital located in Westchester Country about 30 minutes north of New York City. The set, which presents us with a single large interior, suggests a building of grand outer dimensions in the Georgian style, something like a Harvard House. The room we see is used alternately as a dining room, sitting room and for patient-doctor sondultations, as well as for meetings of the entire staff and patient population. It is clean, well-lit, and well-furnished, though not in any way luxurious.

        DANIEL
My fathers are invisible.

        GODOT
I have met them.

        DANIEL
What did you think?

        GODOT
Faithful and true. You know the tune?
(Singing)
   "FAITHFUL AND TRUE..."

DANIEL
Must be disco. That was before my time.

GODOT
Time, time, I stretch myself thin sometimes. And there is Monsieur Malaprop. Come. Sit.

MR. MALAPROP
I like to stand. It is the only exercise you get around here.

GODOT
Up and down, up and down. Such is life.

DANIEL
Mr. Godot?

GODOT
Yes?

DANIEL
When are you leaving?

GODOT
I do not know. Or at least, I haven't been told. In my case, there are more than a few formalities that have to be settled.

MR. MALAPROP
Me, too.

GODOT
They are still trying to find out whether I am alive, and if so, who I am. For them, the name Godot has no reference. The philosophers would say it is an arrow with no target.

DANIEL
I hope to leave today.

MR. MALAPROP
So we all do.

DANIEL
I am planning to go back to my family.

GODOT
I have no family.

MR. MALAPROP
Of course you do. You are Godot.

GODOT
Ah, well. I guess that explains why I'm here.

DANIEL
Your family?

GODOT
Yes.

DANIEL
Oh. Don't they love you?

GODOT
They say they love me.

UNCLE STURTEVANT
(Looking up)
That's what my family says, too.

DANIEL
But you don't have a family.

UNCLE STURTEVANT
The brotherhood of souls is my family.

GODOT
You are lucky.

UNCLE STURTEVANT
I don't see why. After all, I am here with you, and you are all crazy.

MR MALAPROP
The pudding is in the proof.

LUCILLE OUTBACK
I am eighty-proof.

UNCLE STURTEVANT
How else could you stand all those cocktail parties?

LUCILLE OUTBACK
I know, what with the drinks and hors d'oeuvres, and collecting names.

DANIEL
Collecting names?

LUCILLE OUTBACK
Yes. I network - for a living. Names are a salable commodity.

DANIEL
Who do you sell them to?

LUCILLE OUTBACK
The highest bidder.

DANIEL
Is that what brought you here?

LUCILLE OUTBACK
I am here on business. There was one name I hadn't got.

DANIEL
Which one?

(LUCILLE OUTBACK points to GODOT)

DANIEL
Oh. His name is Godot. Everybody has his name already.

UNCLE STURTEVANT
And what good does it do them?

GODOT
Yes, my name is Godot.

LUCILLE OUTBACK
Why, thank you. And what are you doing here?

GODOT
Waiting.

LUCILLE OUTBACK
Waiting? For whom?

GODOT
You.
(All-inclusive)

LUCILLE OUTBACK
What a treat.

GODOT
Some of it has been enjoyable.

MR. MALAPROP
Make a necessity of virtue.

LUCILLE OUTBACK
Only some?

GODOT
Not much.

LUCILLE OUTBACK
Then why? –

GODOT
It has kept me occupied, and I needed the instruction.

LUCILLE OUTBACK
How long? –

GODOT
Oh, here I have been at it a little more than five thousand years.

DANIEL
The dawn of civilization -

LUCILLE OUTBACK
Of man -

MR. MALAPROP
Of woman.
(GODOT smiles)

GODOT
I hope you are not going to spend the sixth millennium asking me questions about the previous five.

DANIEL
Why not? You could play Homer.

GODOT
I was Homer.
(Big pause)

MR. MALAPROP
I knew this was leading somewhere.

UNCLE STURTEVANT
Somewhere is here. Why do you only have one name?

GODOT
It is all I need, as you can see.

MR MALAPROP
Invention is the mother of necessity.

GODOT
Yes.

DANIEL
Well I hope you don't get sprung too soon.

GODOT
At your service, young man.

DANIEL
I need instruction more than you.

GODOT
You are not as old.

DANIEL
No.

GODOT
I can make an impression on you.

DANIEL
If I like.

GODOT
Yes. You will get it from the source. Ah, a nurse. I am rescued.
(NURSE takes GODOT's blood pressure, pulse, and temperature)

NURSE
Fine as always, Mr. Godot.
(GODOT smiles)

GODOT
I am healthy but I am here.

DANIEL
What brought you here?

GODOT
Five policemen and a fire truck.

DANIEL
Sounds exciting.

GODOT
I am sometimes flamboyant.

DANIEL
I love you.

GODOT
That was fast.

DANIEL
You are the father I never had.

GODOT
And the mother, too?

DANIEL
Yes.

GODOT
Well, aren't I the one?

MR. MALAPROP
And the two, too.

GODOT
I thought you had two fathers, A and B.

DANIEL
I am an orphan. They adopted me.

GODOT
So you are adopting me.

DANIEL
Yes.

UNCLE STURTEVANT
That makes sense. We should all choose our own parents.

DANIEL
What if I make a mistake?

GODOT
Correct it: choose again.

UNCLE STURTEVANT
Sounds like marriage.

MR. MALAPROP
Perfect makes practice.

GODOT
I rather like it here, with you.

LADY DALY
You wet-nosed lazy-bones. Get up. Gossip, gossip, gossip. You're worse than that T.V. You could make a living at it, sitting around here all day taking pills and drinking orange juice.

MR. MALAPROP
A sore eye for sight.

LADY DALY
You got it. Now who is going to help me clean up?
(Pause)

GODOT
That's my line.

LADY DALY
You're right about that, Mr. Godot. So you come over here with me...

DANIEL
Look at that.
(ALICE enters)

DANIEL
(Continued)
Hello, Ophelia.

ALICE
That is not my name.

UNCLE STURTEVANT
He was joking. How about helping clean up?
(ALICE sits down and stares at the ceiling)

UNCLE STURTEVANT
Oh.

DANIEL
We all need a rest. Besides, she's a member of the Royal Family.

UNCLE STURTEVANT
So that's why she's here. She was being hounded. It must have been her imagination.

DANIEL
Godot wasn't followed.

MR. MALAPROP
I was. It was a privilege.

ALICE
I have many privileges.

UNCLE STURTEVANT
And no responsibilities? Lady, you've lucked out.

ALICE
I like to dress well.
(All look at her dress, a purple ball-gown)

UNCLE STURTEVANT
Not bad. Whose party is it?

ALICE
This is my casual wear.

UNCLE STURTEVANT
Oh. Seems to me it would attract attention.

ALICE
I wear it everywhere.

UNCLE STURTEVANT
Even...?

ALICE
Yes. That is what ladies-in-waiting are for.

UNCLE STURTEVANT
I don't see –

ALICE
(Ignoring this)
Don't ask personal questions, please. The private functions of royalty are not of any interest to my subjects.

DANIEL
From what I read in the papers, you don't have many private functions left. Anyway, it's pretty obvious that even a queen uses the loo, and a princess -

ALICE
can be here. Yes. Well, let's not discuss it. It is very tiresome, just like you.

LADY DALY
Monsieur Godot, my humble apologies. I had no idea you could clean so well.

GODOT
I have lots of practice. It's a hobby.

LADY DALY
You want a job? I run an agency in my spare time. The good neighborhoods pay diddlypoop and the poor neighborhoods pay much better, don't ask me why.

GODOT
I guess it's a matter of personal pride.

LADY DALY
I guess that's your forte, too.

GODOT
How did you know?

LADY DALY
I know a few things, even if I look dumb.

GODOT
You look beautiful to me. And I won't disparage your brain, either.

LADY DALY
(Beaming)
Mr. Godot, you make me happy.

GODOT
And you, mi'lady, make me laugh.

LADY DALY
Call me Eleanor, sweetie.

GODOT
Yes, Eleanor, sweetie.

LADY DALY
Do you cook too?

GODOT
Sometimes I am the main course.

LADY DALY
I've been told human flesh is somewhat oily.

GODOT
My flesh is not exactly human, and there is enough of it to last indefinitely into the future.

UNCLE STURTEVANT
Cheap trick.

GODOT
Try me.

UNCLE STURTEVANT
(Pausing)
Maybe later.

LADY DALY
I don't have to try.

GODOT
I love the faithful. Unfortunately, most of them inhabit fantasy-land.

LADY DALY
And you are here -

GODOT
I am here.

LADY DALY
Oh.

GODOT
Now. What is for dinner?

ALICE
I'm having -

LADY DALY
You're having what we're having, and it ain't steak.

UNCLE STURTEVANT
Try franks and beans.

LADY DALY
My favorite.

GODOT
Mine, too.

LUCILLE OUTBACK
I would like mine medium rare.

GODOT
At your service.

LUCILLE OUTBACK
Cocktail parties are so fatiguing.

ALICE
The guests are nice.

LADY DALY
They're just as bad as anyone else, but better dressed.

DANIEL
No holes.

LUCILLE OUTBACK
(Yelling)
Don't tell me about gossip. It was all untrue.

LADY DALY
What was untrue?

LUCILLE OUTBACK
That I killed my first husband.
(She breaks down)

LADY DALY
Don't cry, or we'll need an umbrella. Here's a handkerchief. It's all I have, but it's for you.

LUCILLE OUTBACK
All you have?

LADY DALY
They cleaned my clock before I got here. I have nothing and no one.

LUCILLE OUTBACK
I like you.

LADY DALY
Thank you. I like you.

MR. MALAPROP
It's all bridge under the water.

LADY DALY
You said it.

LUCILLE OUTBACK
I am beginning to feel better.

GODOT
One more convert.

DANIEL
To what?

GODOT
Love. Humanity. Depth of soul. Understanding. You see what I mean?

DANIEL
You're a brick.

GODOT
Now don't be saying how wonderful I am. As soon as that begins, everybody starts asking for gifts. On the other hand, when things are going badly, they blame it all on me.

DANIEL
Then why do things go badly?

GODOT
Because I invented the devil.

DANIEL
And why – ?

GODOT
So I could acquire knowledge of evil without myself being or doing evil.

DANIEL
Then -

GODOT
The mess that men make of their lives is due to the devil or his disciples. That is all.

DANIEL
God!

GODOT
Godot!

DANIEL
Will it ever end?

GODOT
You will see.

DANIEL
And his disciples?

GODOT
You will see.

DANIEL
How do I know this is true?

GODOT
First look around you, and tell me what you think.

DANIEL
Eureka! I see a beginning.

GODOT
You are amusing.

DANIEL
So are you.

UNCLE STURTEVANT
I thought I was bad!

GODOT
The difference between us, Uncle Sturtevant, is that the weight of evidence is on my side.

UNCLE STURTEVANT
I am beginning to feel better.

GODOT
Relax. Enjoy yourself.

UNCLE STURTEVANT
Have you cured me?

GODOT
You have cured yourself. All you have to do is see the truth.

UNCLE STURTEVANT
How do you know it when you see it?

GODOT
You feel it - all the way inside. It is the poetry of the soul. It will feed you for a lifetime - for many lifetimes - once you have found it. And you, my dear uncle, have now found it.

UNCLE STURTEVANT
When can I leave here?

GODOT
There are rules. Follow them.

UNCLE STURTEVANT
Dear Mister Godot, I love you.

GODOT
You love yourself, that is why you love me.

(UNCLE STURTEVANT cries)

GODOT
Oh, please, I know you are happy. Anyways, a little megalomania never hurt anybody. It just made you look like a fool. And look at all the fools out there pretending they really are important. Well, they're not. And you are. What you have beats them down cold.

MR. MALAPROP
It's all dam under the water.

LADY DALY
Dinner, dinner, dinner. And I'm hungry, too.

(All inmates line up for trays of food, which they get and take to their seats around the room)

(DR. LANCE HABIT enters. Hidden under a distinguished, not to say imposing, exterior, he is a colossal nincompoop. He is one of those who has gotten to the right place the wrong way)

DR. LANCE HABIT
Well, well, well, are we having lunch?

LUCILLE OUTBACK
Hell, hell, hell, call it brunch.

LADY DALY
Have you had yours today, Dr. Habit?

(GODOT laughs)

DR. LANCE HABIT
Who laughed at me?

GODOT
I did, doctor. I apologize.

DR. LANCE HABIT
Troublemaker.

(All laugh)

DR. LANCE HABIT
Stop! Stop! Godot, you go to the quiet room. Miss Daly, I'll have you put in restraints if you don't shut up. For the rest of you - no grounds privileges till further notice.
(DR. LANCE HABIT leaves)

LADY DALY
I guess he's got pretty potent medicine for those with a sense of humor.

LUCILLE OUTBACK
He can cure everyone but himself.

ALICE
Godot could cure him.
(GODOT is silent)

LADY DALY
Godot is going to the quiet room.

LUCILLE OUTBACK
Solitary -

ALICE
Confinement.
(GODOT smiles)

LADY DALY
Mr. Godot, why do you smile?

GODOT
It will give me an opportunity to pray.

LADY DALY
To whom?

GODOT
The human race.

LADY DALY
Oh.

GODOT
Besides which, I'll fast. I need to lose some poundage, anyways.

LUCILLE OUTBACK
Poor Godot.

MR. MALAPROP
You will be the former self of your shadow.

GODOT
All set-backs are opportunities in disguise.

MR. MALAPROP
All opportunities are setbacks in disguise.

GODOT
Dear Mr. Malaprop, what would we do without your wisdom?

MR. MALAPROP
Eat liver?

ALICE
Yuck.

LADY DALY
Blacks like me like liver. It's cheap and nutritious.

ALICE
I am neither cheap nor nutritious.

LUCILLE OUTBACK
We know you aren't nutritious, my dear. We weren't planning to eat you.

ALICE
Just in case.

LUCILLE OUTBACK
Oh. Well if they give me your liver, I'll see that a suitable donee is found.

DANIEL
By then she'll be smothered in onions.

LUCILLE OUTBACK
My poodle likes liver.

ALICE
Liver, liver, liver! What about getting Godot out of the quiet room?

DANIEL
He seems to like it there. One mattress on the floor, a bare bulb in the ceiling that is always on, and no conveniences. Spartan, I would say.

ALICE
But he's a great personage!

DANIEL
He is great because he is small.

MR. MALAPROP
He is small because he is great.

UNCLE STURTEVANT
We should be like him.

LADY DALY
Let us all be small.
(All laugh, as LADY DALY is quite large)
(Enter DR. LANCE HABIT)

DR. LANCE HABIT
Who is laughing?
(Silence)

DR. LANCE HABIT
(Continued)
Lady Daly, come here. Are you the culprit?

LADY DALY
It's beginning to look like it.

DR. LANCE HABIT
Then you get into quiet room #2. Now!
(She exits)

DR. LANCE HABIT
Any other takers?
(Silence)

DR. LANCE HABIT
(Continued)
Good. You all need discipline, and that's what you'll get. Goodbye.
(DR. LANCE HABIT marches out)

LUCILLE OUTBACK
We have lost our two best lights.
(DOTTIE DUMPLING appearing)

DOTTIE DUMPLING
The dirt here is appalling. I can see Dr. Habit has been around.

LUCILLE OUTBACK
How can you tell?

DOTTIE DUMPLING
Simple. It smells of cigarettes, and patients aren't allowed to smoke.

LUCILLE OUTBACK
A new Sherlock Holmes.

DOTTIE DUMPLING
My name is Dottie Dumpling, and I clean.

DANIEL
Pleased to meet you - I speak for us all.

DOTTIE DUMPLING
You are all very charming.
(Everyone smiles)

DOTTIE DUMPLING
(Continued)
All smiles. Now we can't all be that sick, can we?
(Fewer smiles around)

DOTTIE DUMPLING
(Continued)
Look at my name. First: Dottie. And I'm not Dotty. Second: Dumpling, and I'm thin.

MR. MALAPROP
Don't judge a cover by its book!

DOTTIE DUMPLING
You got it.

A
Then what are we doing here?

DOTTIE DUMPLING
You are just visiting, as is Monsieur Malaprop. The rest of you are involved in some kind of severe imbroglio.

DANIEL
When they admitted me, they said I was suffering from sexual compulsions.

DOTTIE DUMPLING
Nonsense. You're twenty and you're horny. You don't need this place. You need a girl.

ALICE
Well!

DOTTIE DUMPLING
Sorry. I try not to offend, but I didn't know you could overhear.

ALICE
I am a princess of the blood. I never overhear.

UNCLE STURTEVANT
Here they take your blood every day, and they don't care what you hear.

ALICE
Not that blood. My lineage.

UNCLE STURTEVANT
So you have a history. The doctors will be glad to know. How many times have you been in one of these places?

ALICE
(Huffily)
This is my first.

UNCLE STURTEVANT
I suggest you take it for all it's worth. Then you won't have to expand your lineage.

ALICE
I will never come again. It is too humiliating.

MR. MALAPROP
Don't cry. My brain doesn't work either. Life is such.

ALICE
Such what?

UNCLE STURTEVANT
I shall take care of everything.

MR. MALAPROP
The oyster is his world.

ALICE
I am getting confused.

UNCLE STURTEVANT
Declare yourself! Who are you??

ALICE
I don't know. I thought -

MR. MALAPROP
A thought for your pennies.

ALICE
I don't belong here. I am a Princess.

DANIEL
I think, like the rest of us, you have earned a little relaxation from the world.

UNCLE STURTEVANT
Hear, hear.

DOTTIE DUMPLING
I don't hear anything.
(Listening)

ALICE
I think I am going crazy.

UNCLE STURTEVANT
It gets worse.

MR. MALAPROP
It gets better before it gets worse.

ALICE
Hell! Oh, excuse me.

DOTTIE DUMPLING
Here comes Godot, out of the quiet room.

GODOT
Me voici.

ALICE
Enchantée.

MR. MALAPROP
Plus c'est la même chose, plus ça change.
(LADY DALY entering)

LADY DALY
Cut the friggin' French. You ain't a frog.

UNCLE STURTEVANT
How was your stay, Mr. Godot?

GODOT
Very relaxing. You can look at a bare light bulb for hours and not be blinded, quite unlike the sun.

DANIEL
What did you see in this light?

GODOT
A little warmth.

ALICE
Unintended, I promise.

GODOT
Who knows what is ever intended? I look at results. And the result here is that I am back with you, minus a few hours sleep.

DANIEL
No thoughts to share?

GODOT
The light was warm.

DANIEL
But you were locked in.

GODOT
I still am. Only now I have a slightly greater range. I think I shall organize the patients.

UNCLE STURTEVANT
What a novel thought.

GODOT
Not at all. I believe "organization" is a tool of Leninism.

DANIEL
Good God, you're not a follower of Lenin?

GODOT
(Laughing)
Of course not. He was a child of the devil. I just thought we should join hands and see what we can do for ourselves - and others.

DOTTIE DUMPLING
How do you mean, Mr. Godot?

GODOT
Well, you all agree you love me?
(All nod)

GODOT
(Continued)
Yet you don't know who I am?
(All nod)

GODOT
(Continued)
Do you hear what I say?
(Some nod)

GODOT
(Continued)
Can you see what I do?
(Fewer nod)

         GODOT
(Continued)
    And how many wish to do likewise?
(Silence. No nods)

         GODOT
(Continued)
(Smiles)
    Ahh. I am not so popular as I had thought. Habit – not the Doctor but the thing – has a pretty strong grip on people. We shall have to see what we can do to change that.

         ALICE
I don't want to change.

         UNCLE STURTEVANT
Nor I.

         LUCILLE OUTBACK
Nor I.
(General agreement on this point)

         GODOT
I see that Doctor Habit will have to be a pretty good therapist if any of you is ever to get out of here.

         LUCILLE OUTBACK
He gives us pills.

         GODOT
Ah, pills. Is that good?

         UNCLE STURTEVANT
They control my megalomania.

         LUCILLE OUTBACK
And my paranoia.

         LADY DALY
And my aggression.

GODOT
Fantastic. And these pills, do they keep you cured?

LADY DALY
Oh, yes, if you continue to take them.

GODOT
If not?

LUCILLE OUTBACK
You wind up back here.

GODOT
Too bad.
(Everyone agrees it is too bad)

GODOT
(Continued)
I think I shall have to come up with a supplement.

UNCLE STURTEVANT
To what?

GODOT
Your pills.

UNCLE STURTEVANT
Nonsense. Anyway, I am a Sturtevant, descended directly from Peter Stuyvesant, and I don't need pills.

GODOT
Come here.

UNCLE STURTEVANT
Why?

GODOT
I want to look into your eye, close-up.

UNCLE STURTEVANT
Here. What do you see?

GODOT
Pain.

UNCLE STURTEVANT
Phooey.

GODOT
Discord and a faithless son.
(UNCLE STURTEVANT begins to tremble, a little at first, then as dialogue proceeds, violently)

GODOT
(Continued)
Have you wished to kill?
(UNCLE STURTEVANT is silent)

GODOT
(Continued)
Are you afraid of yourself?
(UNCLE STURTEVANT shakes violently)

GODOT
(Continued)
You do not need pills. You need love, including the love you threw away on your son.

UNCLE STURTEVANT
Oh, God.

GODOT
No, Godot. At least get my name right.
(Smiles all around)

DR. LANCE HABIT
(Entering)
What's going on here?

A
Since I am only a visitor, I shall speak for what I have seen.

Godot here has cured Uncle Sturtevant of his megalomania by putting a mirror up to the face of his own tragedy.

GODOT
Uncle Sturtevant has been wounded in his heart. I have helped to make him better.

DR. LANCE HABIT
Nonsense. Uncle Sturtevant will get better when I say so, not before. I am the Doctor, not you, Mr. Godot, or anyone else.

A
I am a witness –

DR. LANCE HABIT
You are a visitor and nothing else. So visit and then leave.
(A shuts up)
(DR. LANCE HABIT leaves)

MR. MALAPROP
A rose is a rose.

ALICE
Gertrude Stein goes both ways indiscriminately!

GODOT
I think she only went one way - and that was alright.

DANIEL
I like girls.

GODOT
Don't protest too much or we'll begin to wonder.
(DANIEL loses face)

GODOT
(Continued)
Well, well, well, you'll be out of here soon, diagnosis, pills and all, and then you can have as many girlfriends as you please. There is no shortage of girls, only of time, and you are young – and I am not.

DANIEL
How old are you?

GODOT
As old as this earth. In fact, older. This is just my most recent incarnation.

A
If you said such things outside, they would lock you up.
(*GODOT gestures: here I am*)

A
Oh.

LUCILLE OUTBACK
I will put you up for a club when we get out.

GODOT
But you are a woman, and you club is single - sex.

LUCILLE OUTBACK
Well, my husband will put you up for his club.

GODOT
But it is exclusionary, and I am by nature inclusive.

LUCILLE OUTBACK
Don't be difficult. Everybody is entitled to have his own circle of friends.

MR. MALAPROP
Choose and pick, choose and pick.

GODOT
What if you like everybody?

UNCLE STURTEVANT
What if everybody likes you?

GODOT
It would be hard to justify exclusivity in that case.

LUCILLE OUTBACK
This is too much for me.
(Lies back in a chair)
I don't mean to do anyone harm.

GODOT
The only one you harm is yourself. Open up your life, it will make more than yourself happy.

LUCILLE OUTBACK
Oh, I am feeling better. The paranoia seems to be lifting.

GODOT
You can say goodbye to it, Lucille. You are free of your presumptions.

DR. LANCE HABIT
(Walking in)
Will you stop curing people, Mr. Godot? That is my province, not yours. While you're at it, you might try curing yourself.

GODOT
What is wrong with me, Doctor?

DR. LANCE HABIT
You are a manic-depressive with paranoid affect. You sit in flower-beds, you speak in non-sequiturs, you stop traffic in the middle of Times Square, you walk through Harlem at eleven at night, and through Central Park at twelve, you hike from Battery Park to Yonkers in your socks when it is raining, and so on. Is this normal?

GODOT
It is playful, and definitely not normal. But it had its purpose.

DR. LANCE HABIT
And what was that?

GODOT

To hone my will, and to focus your attention, both of which I have done.

DR. LANCE HABIT

(Furious)

I shall prescribe some thorazine for you tomorrow morning. You are obviously out of control.

GODOT

You are the one who is out of control, Doctor. I have always known what I was doing.

DR. LANCE HABIT

You are a fraud, Mr. Godot!

GODOT

And you are a Doctor, Dr. Habit. I hope there are not many like you.

DR. LANCE HABIT

Quiet! Or I shall put you in seclusion.

(GODOT says nothing. His face becomes impassive)

DR. LANCE HABIT

Oh!

(DR. LANCE HABIT exits)

LADY DALY

He reminds me of my boyfriend. Dr. Godot - I mean Mr. Godot - when they bite, you bite back.

GODOT

One day in seclusion is enough for now, Lady Daly. But if we all - all of us - bite back, some good may come of it.

ALICE

Oh, Mr. Godot!

GODOT
An admirer already.

ALICE
Don't you love me?

GODOT
I am spread pretty thin at the moment.

ALICE
I'll wait.

GODOT
But I'm not royal, not even noble.

ALICE
I can arrange things.

GODOT
Why not you become a commoner? All you have to do is renounce your title.

ALICE
Renounce my title!? It is all I have!

GODOT
Not at all. You are attractive and talented and moderately intelligent. Even without a title you would have a lineage.

ALICE
But I would have to earn a living.

GODOT
Worse things can happen. Anyhow, a title is a burden. It involves you in a whole hypocritical charade of trying to be what you are not - human. Well, throw it out the window and assume your humanity. Then you can be whatever you are. I am certainly no prince and have no desire to be.

ALICE
Oh, Mr. Godot, my title is myself. I cannot give it up.

GODOT
As you choose. I cannot choose for you. I can only help you see what the possibilities are.

MR. MALAPROP
Mr. Godot, why are we mad?

GODOT
I suppose some of us are sick. Illness comes in many forms, and this is one of them. Why, for the present, I cannot say. But you will learn why soon enough.

A
Daniel, why are you here?

DANIEL
It is someone's sorry joke.

A
But are you ill?

DANIEL
I don't think so. At least I didn't feel ill till they started treating me. Now I feel wretched.

A
We'll get you out of here in no time.

DANIEL
Try.

A
Where is that Doctor Habit? What an awful name.

DANIEL
There are nice doctors, but mine is Habit.

A
What's his first name?

DANIEL
Lance.

MR. MALAPROP
There's a name in nothing.

A
I should say there are lots of names in nothing.

DANIEL
God knows what parents will cook up.

A
You don't look sick.

DANIEL
Looks are not very reliable in this department.

A
You seem coherent.

DANIEL
Ask me how I feel.

A
How do you feel?

DANIEL
Crazy. I am being followed, my mail is opened, my apartment is bugged, my pills are poisoned, my shower scalds at odd moments, rumors about me float all over New York, - none of them true - my private life is made public, my poetry is constantly rejected on the weakest of pretexts, those who know me collude; in short, my entire life has slipped out of my control.

    A
Now I see why you are here. Is any of this true?

    DANIEL
You tell me.

    A
Well, I don't think so. But finding evidence for what you say could not be easy.

    DANIEL
Impossible.

    A
Then let's leave it alone and proceed from here.

    DANIEL
Yes?

    A
How long have you been here?

    DANIEL
Two weeks.

    A
You'll need at least another two to get out.

    DANIEL
Remember, my doctor is Habit.

    A
Give it another four weeks.

    DANIEL
Eeeow!

    A
Your problems are not minor.

    DANIEL
I shouldn't have said anything. It always gets me in trouble.

A
Oh, Daniel, I wish so much to help you. If you do what the doctor says, you'll be out soon.

DANIEL
That Doctor?

A
Do you have another?

DANIEL
Saints preserve me.

GODOT
I suppose they will.

DANIEL
Mr. Godot, am I going to die?

GODOT
(Laughs)
Daniel, we are all going to die. The question is, then what?

DANIEL
Well?

GODOT
Those who have made the right choices will continue to live here or elsewhere, as one thing or another; those who have made the wrong choices will be reduced to nothing.

DANIEL
Nothing?

GODOT
Nothing.

DANIEL
But what is nothing?

GODOT
Nothing does not exist.

DANIEL
Oh.

GODOT
Think about it.

DANIEL
I'll try.

GODOT
You'll succeed. Any other questions?
(There are none)

GODOT
(Continued)
I wish all my assignments were so easy.

ALICE
But this is a mental hospital.

GODOT
Yes.

ALICE
Oh.

GODOT
Life – parents, friends, guardians – have softened you up for the kill.

ALICE
And we were killed.

GODOT
Exactly. And here I am trying to bring you back into life. You may have made foolish choices, but you were never wicked.

LADY DALY
What next?

GODOT
I suppose they'll patch you up and send you on out to get knocked down again.

LUCILLE OUTBACK
I have a social worker.

GODOT
A band-aid on a severe wound to the head.

LADY DALY
Then what are we supposed to do?

MR. MALAPROP
Easy go as easy come.

GODOT
Monsieur Malaprop, you are a dream.
(MR. MALAPROP tips his hat)

GODOT
(Continued)
I am trying to think of a plan of action that will redeem us all. But, then, I never do anything premeditated.

LUCILLE OUTBACK
Never?

GODOT
Well, hardly ever.

UNCLE STURTEVANT
And he is hardly ever sick at sea.

GODOT
I never go to sea.

UNCLE STURTEVANT
All the better. You can be sick here.

GODOT
Here I am.

LADY DALY
But you are not sick.

GODOT
Words, words, words:
So you think you are tough?
You are going to make me unhappy?
You are going to beat me up?
I have a better idea than you.
I shall think you into a pit,
Where a black lantern will be lit,
Shining on your frightened eyes,
And no one will pay attention
To your cries;
I shall put your hat on you ass-
Backwards, and make you walk
Cross-legged like a crow
Into a road full of trucks,
Which will run on your toes,
Crushing them. O, joy!
Punishment for my pain!
Vindication of shame!
Will you ever try,
You black-eared toad,
To knock me down again?
Even I can play a tune or two.

ALICE
That was very good, Mr. Godot. I wish I could write like that.

LADY DALY
I wish I could speak like that.

GODOT
You can. Just listen to yourself.

LADY DALY
Fellow citizens of the World, rescue yourselves from the forces of Impotence. Steal back your lives! Turn the tables on adversity! Find love where it does not lie! You are free to wish what you want and then to make it come true. Help yourselves – no one else knows how, as well as you. I love you all!

GODOT
Lady Daly, I could not have said it better. You were born with a silver spoon in your mouth.

LADY DALY
But I am a black overweight manic-depressive.

GODOT
You are my friend, and I am your audience whenever you need one.

LADY DALY
Oh, Mr. Godot, I fail you at every turn.

GODOT
No, you are successful whenever you exercise your will. Just do so in the right direction, and marvels will appear.

LUCILLE OUTBACK
Oh, Mr. Godot…

GODOT
Yes!

LUCILLE OUTBACK
May I be good, too?

GODOT
This is not an exclusive club.

MR. MALAPROP
Read David Copperfield.

UNCLE STURTEVANT
Or Shakespeare.

GODOT
Whatever.

LADY DALY
You mean no one is excluded from happiness?

GODOT
Of course not. That would serve no purpose except to play into the hands of the forces of evil.

UNCLE STURTEVANT
Ahh!

GODOT
Please close your mouth, Uncle Sturtevant. I am not a dentist.

UNCLE STURTEVANT
Well I am, and you perform the most delicate extractions in the most artful way.

GODOT
I am an artist in my spare time.

LUCILLE OUTBACK
Oh, what kind?

GODOT
Performance artist.

LUCILLE OUTBACK
I haven't heard of that.

GODOT
It blossomed in the sixties. Now it's a bit passé, but I keep my end up.

LUCILLE OUTBACK
May I watch you sometime?

GODOT
You are.

LUCILLE OUTBACK
Oh, this is fascinating.

GODOT
It's work, and I am glad to have it.

LUCILLE OUTBACK
So many actors are out of work.

GODOT
The theatrical profession is under-utilized. I wonder why?

UNCLE STURTEVANT
Supply and demand.

LUCILLE OUTBACK
Gross commercialization.

ALICE
Exploitation.

MR. MALAPROP
I think we are all being ridden for a take.

GODOT
Ah, Mr. Malaprop, right again.
(They bow to one another)

GODOT
Yes, and art is hard.

ALICE
Ars longa, vita brevis.

GODOT
That would be a good one for Mr. Malaprop.

ALICE
He doesn't know Latin.

GODOT
How do you?

ALICE
I may be a princess, but I have a brain.

GODOT
At last. Now we know your problem.

ALICE
You're right! I feel better already. Oh, Mr. Godot, thank you.

GODOT
Thank yourself. Everyone here has the wherewithal to cure themselves. It is a matter of will properly directed. Just think, you may all set yourselves free!

ALL
Oh, Mr. Godot, we love you.

GODOT
Let's keep it quiet. Habit may reappear.

ALICE
Habit or habit?

GODOT
Either one; they're both deadly.

ALICE
Oh.

UNCLE STURTEVANT
But what if we can't stick to our new régime?

GODOT
You want an instant replay?
(All say no)
Thank you. You get what you ask for.

DANIEL
Then how do we get out of here?

GODOT
You are well. Just behave, and they'll let you go. After all, though Dr. Habit runs the place, not even he can keep you here if you're demonstrably cured.

LADY DALY
Oh, Mr. Godot. You are a peach!

DANIEL
Yes, Mr. Godot, but you are here, and it seems you have always been well.

GODOT
I have my moments.

DOTTIE DUMPLING
Of inspiration.

GODOT
I have my slack times, too. Right now, I am resting.

DANIEL
I wonder what you're like when you're at work?

GODOT
Dazzling.

LADY DALY
We can't wait.

GODOT
As I say, I am resting. After that…?

LADY DALY
After that we put you on a float in Macy's Thanksgiving Day Parade.

GODOT
That's a bit conspicuous. I might become a target for the world's malcontents.

DANIEL
Amongst others.

GODOT
Let us tread softly, and watch out for other peoples' toes.

LADY DALY
You aren't any fun.

GODOT
Be patient, Lady Daly. We will have fun, but we must get our timing right.

DANIEL
Otherwise, all is for naught.

GODOT
There you are.

ACT II

SCENE 1

Same scene, some two weeks later.

        LUCILLE OUTBACK
I thought we were going to be at home by now.

        UNCLE STURTEVANT
Me too. I think someone is conspiring to keep us here.

        LUCILLE OUTBACK
Wait. I'm paranoid.

        UNCLE STURTEVANT
And I'm in charge.

        LUCILLE OUTBACK
Then you must know why we're all still here.

        MR. MALAPROP
Better never than late.

        LUCILLE OUTBACK
What does that mean?

        UNCLE STURTEVANT
He's always wrong - or right - I don't know which.

        DANIEL
Mr. Godot, why are we still here?

GODOT
Because in your present state you would not last more than five minutes outside.

UNCLE STURTEVANT
I feel well.

DANIEL
Me, too.

GODOT
That is no indication of your state of health. You must be up and about, go for walks through the gardens, cook, sing, play dominoes or ping pong, and so on. And you must talk to your doctor and help him to understand what's troubling you, what brought you here. When they know that, then you will be on your way home.

DOTTIE DUMPLING
I don't want to go home.

LADY DALY
Don't worry, Dottie, you can come live with me.

DOTTIE DUMPLING
I want my job back.

GODOT
I am sure you will have it back, Dottie. The doctor's methods may seem harsh, but in fact they perform miracles. I am sure you will be back to work soon.

LADY DALY
How do you know that?

GODOT
What was I supposed to say?

LADY DALY
Oh.

GODOT

I cannot wish us all out of here. That would just put us all out in the street with the same problems that bedevil us here. Our stay would have been for nothing.

MR. MALAPROP

Nothing is as nothing does.

GODOT

It is just like life: if we do not ask the right questions, we do not get the right answers.

DANIEL

What is the right question?

GODOT

Well?

LADY DALY

Why we are here?

GODOT

And?

DANIEL

To discover what it is we do not know.

GODOT

And then you will be prepared.

LADY DALY

For what?

GODOT

For what comes on the other side of life.

DANIEL

What if you're not ready?

GODOT

Then you have another go round.

LADY DALY
And another and another -

DANIEL
Until you learn your lesson.

UNCLE STURTEVANT
Sounds vaguely Asiatic to me.

GODOT
Uncle Sturtevant, you are a winner.

UNCLE STURTEVANT
Always thought so.

MR. MALAPROP
Mother is the necessity of invention.

GODOT
I am not so sure. Anyway, right now we must cooperate.

LUCILLE OUTBACK
Collaborate.

LADY DALY
Give in.

DANIEL
Capitulate.

ALICE
Quit.

MR. MALAPROP
Lance, Dr. Habit.
(Enter DR. HABIT with some STUDENT DOCTORS and some NURSES)

DR. LANCE HABIT
Time for a community meeting.
(All move chairs in semi-circle facing audience)

DR. LANCE HABIT
(Continued)
Let us begin. To begin with, I have bad news. Douglas Pinckney, who left us two weeks ago, has committed suicide.

(Silence)

DR. LANCE HABIT
(Continued)
Does no one have a reaction?

(Silence)

DR. LANCE HABIT
(Continued)
Well, for those of you in a similar position, I would point out that shifting the burden of guilt onto the shoulders of those who survive you will not work. Some of us may grieve, but we all eventually get on with our lives.

UNCLE STURTEVANT
Dr. Habit, we do not kill ourselves to inspire guilt in others or in you. We do it because we are in pain, and there is no other way out.

LADY DALY
We are not here because we want to punish someone, except perhaps ourselves.

ALICE
I am here because of a failure in love.

DR. LANCE HABIT
Good cause for pain, my dear.

ALICE
You know nothing about pain, Dr. Habit.

LADY DALY
So shut up.

DR. LANCE HABIT
Miss Daly –

LADY DALY
Lady to you.

DR. LANCE HABIT
Lady Daly, you must control yourself, or you will be back in the quiet room.

LADY DALY
Appropriate.

DR. LANCE HABIT
I warn you.

GODOT
And pain, Dr. Habit, where does this pain come from?

DR. LANCE HABIT
I suppose from experience.

GODOT
Then why are some here and some not?

DR. LANCE HABIT
Because some of us know how to protect ourselves.

GODOT
Do you teach that here?

DR. LANCE HABIT
Health is the best preventative.

GODOT
Very good. Do you know pain, Dr. Habit?

DR. LANCE HABIT
I think so.

GODOT
Ah. It is hard to teach what one does not know.
(Silence)

GODOT
(Continued)
Mrs. Outback, why are you here?

LUCILLE OUTBACK
I am afraid.

GODOT
Again? I thought we had cured you.

LUCILLE OUTBACK
I am having a relapse.

GODOT
You will certainly engage Dr. Habit for a while.

LUCILLE OUTBACK
I have. And it is time for me to go.

GODOT
But has Dr. Habit freed you of your fears?

LUCILLE OUTBACK
No. He has added to them.

GODOT
How?

LUCILLE OUTBACK
Now I am afraid of him.

GODOT
How helpful. How did he do this?

LUCILLE OUTBACK
He prescribed an overdose of medications for me.

GODOT
Why?

LUCILLE OUTBACK
Because he was afraid of me.

GODOT
And why should he be afraid of you? Why should anybody be afraid of you?

LUCILLE OUTBACK
Because I know.

GODOT
Know?

LUCILLE OUTBACK
Things.

GODOT
Things?
(Silence)

GODOT
(Continued)
Well, we'll leave the rest up to your medical team, and they can discuss it with Dr. Habit, who no doubt has lots to say.

LADY DALY
Life is so fatiguing.

GODOT
Why is that, Lady Daly?

LADY DALY
I barely sleep, because my roommate is always spying on me.

GODOT
Is paranoia part of your diagnosis?

LADY DALY
I don't know, but she is spying.

GODOT
We'll have to talk to the nurses.

LADY DALY
If you can find one that is not spying. I'll look into it for you. Now, what brought you here?

LADY DALY
Mania. I beat up my boyfriend.

GODOT
I guess he's not as big as you.

LADY DALY
He's a punk, but I love him.

GODOT
Then why did you beat him up?

LADY DALY
He was out of line.

GODOT
Seems reasonable. Did you tell anyone here?

LADY DALY
When I was admitted, yes.

GODOT
Something seems to have been lost in the transmission. You should talk to your doctors. I think you are supposed to be manic.

LADY DALY
I take my pills.

GODOT
Well, you seem alright to me. Talk to your team.

LADY DALY
Team, team, what's a team?

LUCILLE OUTBACK
Honey, those are the people that look after you here.

LADY DALY
Well, I hope they let me go home soon.

GODOT
So do we.

DR. LANCE HABIT
I think our community meeting has been hijacked.

GODOT
Excuse me.

DR. LANCE HABIT
Does anyone other than Mr. Godot care to ask a question?

DOTTIE DUMPLING
Yes. Why do you dislike us?
(DR. LANCE HABIT at a loss)

DOTTIE DUMPLING
Is it because we are black or Hispanic or simply people of no means?

DR. LANCE HABIT
Nonsense. I do like you, I am very fond of you.

LUCILLE OUTBACK
Then why are you so autocratic?

DR. LANCE HABIT
I didn't realize...

LUCILLE OUTBACK
Well, now you do.

ALICE
You are not helping us.

LUCILLE OUTBACK
You make my paranoia worse.

UNCLE STURTEVANT

With you around, I have to think I'm God just to protect myself. You may think I like it, but I don't. I would rather be anything than God.

DR. LANCE HABIT

I am sorry.

(Silence)

MR. MALAPROP

All ends well that is well.

A

Well, I'm well and I want to get out of here.

DR. LANCE HABIT

What are your symptoms?

DANIEL

He's with me.

DR. LANCE HABIT

Oh.

DANIEL

He's one of my fathers.

DR. LANCE HABIT

How many do you have?

A

Two. Me and Mr. Malaprop.

DANIEL

Oh! B! You here too!

MR. MALAPROP

It's hard to understand, but very easy to believe.

DR. LANCE HABIT

I'm going crazy.

                    GODOT
Reality looks like that sometimes.

                MR. MALAPROP
You look like the canary that ate the cat.

                    GODOT
So we all do.
(General merriment)

                    GODOT
(To DR. LANCE HABIT)
   Well?

                DR. LANCE HABIT
You are all discharged!
(Everyone dances)

ACT II

SCENE 2

The gardens outside the hospital. It is September and sunny and very beautiful. The former patients are out for a stroll. It is at least a month since they were "discharged."

      DANIEL
Funny. I always wanted to leave. Now I want to stay.

      LUCILLE OUTBACK
There is no staff. When Dr. Habit discharged us, there was no reason for them to stay.

      LADY DALY
Now we have a home, a nice home.

      DOTTIE DUMPLING
For free.

      GODOT
We must keep it up, or it will fall down.

      ALICE
We don't want that to happen.

      GODOT
So long as we stay here, it won't.

ALICE
I am applying for a job in town.

UNCLE STURTEVANT
What job?

ALICE
As a waitress.

UNCLE STURTEVANT
Are you crazy! You're a princess.

ALICE
Mr. Godot said that titles are empty labels, and I agree. To be a princess does not guarantee you are good, or anything else, I think.

LADY DALY
My name is Lady, and we know I live up to it.

ALICE
Well I could not live up to being a princess, so I have quit.

UNCLE STURTEVANT
And now you're a waitress.
(He laughs)

LUCILLE OUTBACK
I like to think I'm somebody.

LADY DALY
You are, but around here it doesn't count for much.

ALICE
Maybe you should be a waitress, too, Lucille.

LUCILLE OUTBACK
What does it pay?

ALICE
It depends on the tips. If you are polite and kind without being forward, you will be rewarded.

LUCILLE OUTBACK
Oh. Well -

ALICE
I'll take you down tomorrow. I'm sure they have room.

GODOT
Uncle Sturtevant!

UNCLE STURTEVANT
Yes.

GODOT
Still musing over immortality?

UNCLE STURTEVANT
Yes. And the Greatness of Being.

GODOT
Heavy - duty.

UNCLE STURTEVANT
Yes.

GODOT
Where does it all lead?

UNCLE STURTEVANT
Into the dark.

GODOT
Do you see in the dark?

UNCLE STURTEVANT
That is what I have been trying to do for some time now.

GODOT
How do you get out?

UNCLE STURTEVANT
By finding my courage.

GODOT
Yes?

UNCLE STURTEVANT
It is hard to live with the truth about yourself. Sometimes it seems easier just to run away.

GODOT
But it is not easier, is it?

UNCLE STURTEVANT
No. I cannot run away forever. A little pain now saves a lot of pain later.

GODOT
You cannot lie to yourself forever.

UNCLE STURTEVANT
I am tired of lies. I want my life back.

GODOT
Then you will have it. And your brain, too. Look at me. I am the one you are seeking. Can you tell?

UNCLE STURTEVANT
Yes. The truth is in your eyes, whenever I look.

GODOT
I am only Godot, and you see right through me.

UNCLE STURTEVANT
(Breaking down)
Oh, Mr. Godot, I don't see how I can do without you, without somebody. I am so alone.

GODOT
So am I.
(GODOT looks very sad)

UNCLE STURTEVANT
You, alone?

GODOT
More so than anyone else.
(UNCLE STURTEVANT is blowing his nose)

GODOT
(Continued)
Feel better?

UNCLE STURTEVANT
Yes. Mr. Godot, who are you?

GODOT
It is difficult to say, and for now inappropriate to discuss.

UNCLE STURTEVANT
How can anyone live without you?
(GODOT gestures around himself)

GODOT
Things seem to be improving from what they were.

ALICE
I wonder why.

MR. MALAPROP
Mother is the necessity of invention.

GODOT
It is not mere invention, Mr. Malaprop. People have begun to do the right thing.

LUCILLE OUTBACK
We are setting ourselves free.

DOTTIE DUMPLING
Of what?

LUCILLE OUTBACK
Past injury.

DANIEL
Yes, now even I have a future to live for.

A & B
And we can still live for each other and set Daniel free.

LUCILLE OUTBACK
I feel so invigorated. I think I shall go out and chop down a tree.

UNCLE STURTEVANT
I'll help. But make sure it's not cherry. We want history behind us – and our future ahead.

GODOT
It seems to be a little damp out here.

MR. MALAPROP
Rain is right.

GODOT
I suppose it is. I am beginning to feel very weak. My will seems to be softening, and my sight shows me nothing. Now I am no more than human.

DANIEL
Mr. Godot, what is wrong?

GODOT
Nothing is wrong, Daniel. It is just that I have done my good deed, and now I have become what I had chosen to be.

DANIEL
What is that?

GODOT
A man.

LADY DALY
Oh, Mr. Godot!

GODOT
That is all I am now, and just as vulnerable as the rest of you.

DOTTIE DUMPLING
You still give good advice.

GODOT
Now it is up to you to give good advice, even to yourselves. You have seen me in action, now go out and practice it.

MR. MALAPROP
Preach what you practice.

GODOT
That, too, Mr. Malaprop. The right word can often save a situation.

DOTTIE DUMPLING
How can we save yours, Mr. Godot?

GODOT
Save yourselves and I shall be saved. That is all I can say. Now I must go. We all have a little housecleaning to do, even me. Oh, God.

(GODOT falls on the ground in front of the entire cast and begins to have convulsion. At the same time he calls out:)
I love you, I love you, I love you.
(The convulsions grow more intense until GODOT is screaming in agony and still repeating "I love you". Finally, there is a peak in his pain and the convulsions subside and GODOT falls silent. Everyone present is amazed, but not embarrassed)
Ohhh.

DOTTIE DUMPING
Are you alright, Mr. Godot?

GODOT
Yes, Dottie. Are you?

DOTTIE DUMPLING
Oh, yes, Mr. Godot. I was afraid you would die. Did you?

GODOT
No, Dottie. I am still alive. But I think there is one less personage present amongst our number.

DOTTIE DUMPLING
Who is that, Mr. Godot?

GODOT
The devil.
(Much attention given to this by witnesses)

GODOT
I have taken him back to where he came from.

A
Where is that, Mr. Godot?

GODOT
To nothing. He has been reduced to nothing.

A
Then what is left?

GODOT
A mess. Each one of us must clean up his mess.

MR. MALAPROP
"If everyone swept his own threshold, the world would be clean." Goethe.

DOTTIE DUMPLING
After that, Mr. Godot?

GODOT
After that, Dottie, we really are in Heaven.

DOTTIE DUMPLING
Oh, Mr. Godot!
(All present swarm around GODOT)

ACT III

SCENE 1

As in Act I, some months later.

    DANIEL
I wonder what has become of Dr. Habit?

    GODOT
He is hanging from a large apple tree in the patients' orchard.

    DANIEL
Suicide?
(GODOT nods yes)

    DANIEL
(Continued)
Wonder who diagnosed him?

    GODOT
It was a self-diagnosis.

    DANIEL
I guess it was accurate.

    GODOT
Yes.

    DANIEL
What about the other doctors and nurses?

GODOT
I think they survived the liberation.

DANIEL
But they're not here?

GODOT
No. It was not congenial to them.

DANIEL
And the patients?

GODOT
They come and go.

DANIEL
Yes.
(Some patients come and go)

GODOT
Do you know who I am?

DANIEL
You are Godot.

GODOT
Yes. But do you know who Godot is?

DANIEL
Of course.

GODOT
And I don't frighten you?

DANIEL
No. I like you.

GODOT
I like you.

DANIEL
Yes.

GODOT
I am older than you.

DANIEL
It doesn't show.

GODOT
No. I am even older than your father.

DANIEL
It doesn't show.

GODOT
I like you very much.

DANIEL
Me, too.
(They kiss once lightly, then once passionately)

DANIEL
(Continued)
What are all the women going to say?

GODOT
They know what it means to have a man.

DANIEL
Have you ever loved a woman?

GODOT
Of course.

DANIEL
Then -

GODOT
This is a first for me.

DANIEL
Me, too. I wonder what A and B will say.

UNCLE STURTEVANT
Any room for me?

GODOT
Monogamy is the best policy. That excludes you.

UNCLE STURTEVANT
Isn't it the way. I guess I'll have to try one of the ladies.

DOTTIE DUMPLING
(Looking alluring)
Hello, Uncle Sturtevant.

UNCLE STURTEVANT
Uh-oh. The human bean-sprout.

GODOT
Do not hurt others' feelings, Uncle Sturtevant. Yours are on the line, too.

UNCLE STURTEVANT
Oh. Well, Dottie, you are looking ravishing.

DOTTIE DUMPLING
I've been practicing.

UNCLE STURTEVANT
With Godot here?

DOTTIE DUMPLING
By myself.

UNCLE STURTEVANT
Very good policy. That's my method, too. But when one is ready for company -

DOTTIE DUMPLING
I am.

UNCLE STURTEVANT
I am, too.

(DOTTIE DUMPLING and UNCLE STURTEVANT kiss)

GODOT

I wonder if Cupid has taken up his cudgels.

(LUCILLE OUTBACK enters, saying)

LUCILLE OUTBACK

I have never heard of this Sappho; is she in the Social Register?

ALICE

(Following)

I think she antedates the Social Register. She owned an island off Greece called Lesbos.

LUCILLE OUTBACK

A big island?

ALICE

Huge.

LUCILLE OUTBACK

I would like to make her acquaintance.

ALICE

For the present, you'll have to settle for me.

LUCILLE OUTBACK

For what?

ALICE

For love.

LUCILLE OUTBACK

What love?

ALICE

My love.

LUCILLE OUTBACK

You love me? Where is Godot?

GODOT
Here, Lucille.

LUCILLE OUTBACK
What is this about love?

GODOT
What love?

LUCILLE OUTBACK
Alice has declared herself.

GODOT
Give her a kiss. That is the appropriate thing to do.

LUCILLE OUTBACK
But Mr. Godot, don't you see, she is a woman.

GODOT
Everyone knows that. And so are you.

LUCILLE OUTBACK
But I can't kiss a woman.

GODOT
Try.
(She tries, successfully)

ALICE
I have been practicing on Lady Daly.

LUCILLE OUTBACK
When the walls of Jericho fall, they crash.
(ALICE and LUCILLE OUTBACK kiss again)
(A and B enter)

A
Looks like the sexual revolution has finally taken off.

B
Taken off what?

A
You name it, here it is.

B
But what about Lady Daly?
(LADY DALY enters looking very forlorn)

LADY DALY
I've lost my horse.

A
Mare or stallion?

LADY DALY
Stallion. They give you the better ride.

B
Whatever happened to Dr. Habit?

LADY DALY
He's got a good seat.

GODOT
He hung himself. Over there.

LADY DALY
Is he dead yet?

GODOT
I forgot to look.

DANIEL
I'll take his pulse.
(DANIEL does so)

DANIEL
Cut him down, he's alive.
(Everyone gathers around HABIT, who comes to)

DR. LANCE HABIT
(Looking around)
I must be in Hell.

DANIEL
We are angels, you are not.

DOTTIE DUMPLING
We just saved you.

LADY DALY
For me.

DR. LANCE HABIT
God!

GODOT
Godot.

LADY DALY
Now it's my turn for a kiss.
(She administers one smack on HABIT's lips)
If you're going to be my husband, you're going to have to change your name. Your present cognomen does not apply.
(To everyone)
Any suggestions?
(Silence)

LADY DALY
(Continued)
Good. Then I choose – Lancelot Brown. You have the name, I am the number.
(She indicates the color of her skin)

BROWN
You're my wife?

LADY DALY
I'm the only one here who knows how to handle you.

BROWN
Oh, shit.

LADY DALY
You stop that right now. You don't know how lucky you are. You may be a doctor, but I am a patient, and that makes me your superior. Furthermore, we have abolished doctors here. They are superfluous, as everyone is well. If no one is sick, who needs welfare? Get up! Now it's my turn. Give me a kiss.

(BROWN *does so*)

LADY DALY
(*Continued*)
Honey, I'm going to call you Lord. Together we should do better than the Prince and Princess of Wales.

BROWN
I never thought I would conclude an interracial marriage.

GODOT
Many strange things are happening, all of them admirable.

BROWN
What would my mother say?

DOTTIE DUMPLING
I am sure she'd be pleased. Lady Daly is no dishrag. I would like to be a Lady, too.

GODOT
That can be arranged. Any other volunteers?

(*Everyone volunteers*)

GODOT
Before we all jump over the bridge, let me point out that privilege entails responsibility. How many of you want responsibility?

DANIEL
For what?

GODOT
Anything other than yourselves.

DOTTIE DUMPLING
I have trouble enough with myself.

LADY DALY
Me, too.
(All agree)

GODOT
Then I think titles would be inappropriate.

LADY DALY
Except for me.

GODOT
Lady Daly, your title is not a title, it is a name. Keep it well polished.

LADY DALY
Ok.

GODOT
Thank you. Dr. Habit, how do you feel? I mean Mr. Brown.

BROWN
About what?

GODOT
The state of the world.

BROWN
From here it looks distinctly more promising than previously.
(All agree)

GODOT
Could you tell me why?

BROWN
Because we love one another for what we are, not for what we are not.

GODOT
What comes next?
(BROWN is at a loss)

GODOT
(Continued)
Anybody?
(Silence)

DANIEL
We all love one another equally.

GODOT
You are brash for your age – and correct. Then?

DANIEL
Each one of us cleans up his mess.

DOTTIE DUMPLING
That's my line.

GODOT
It's correct. Thank you, both. So?
(Everybody goes about tidying up. The telephones are very busy as each inmate must account for a lot of bad past practices. Finally:)

GODOT
Are we ready?

DOTTIE DUMPLING
For what?

GODOT
This you must take on faith. Are we ready?
(All nod yes)

(There is a period of darkness, then light reappears on a cast outfitted each with a pair of wings)

    GODOT

You are now raised to the rank of angels. Do not fall down. The world as you have known it is Hell, and no one who has known it and survived wants to repeat the experience. Am I right?

(All nod yes)

    DOTTIE DUMPLING

What do we do now?

    GODOT

Meet your neighbors. Anyone you pick will serve as your guide.

    DOTTIE DUMPLING

Are we dead?

    GODOT

My dear Dottie, now you are truly alive.

    DANIEL

Can we ever go back?

    GODOT

Do the right thing and you will never have to.

    BROWN

Or want to. Purgatory is not pleasant.

    DANIEL

Is the world still there?

    GODOT

Forget the world. It has already forgotten you.

    DANIEL

What do we do in Heaven?

GODOT
Whatever good you can imagine.

A
That will keep us busy for awhile.

GODOT
Imagination is infinite, so your business should last an eternity.

DANIEL
I think I'll go study infinitesimals.

DOTTIE DUMPLING
I shall dust.

LADY DALY
I'm going to work out.

A & B
We will do what we do best: wait for Godot.

GODOT
I shall keep you waiting.

DOTTIE DUMPLING
I shall preen my wings.

ALICE
I shall help you.

UNCLE STURTEVANT
I shall trust everyone.

BROWN
I shall become a patient. I need to relax.

LADY DALY
Darling.

DANIEL
The world is beginning to recede from sight.

      A
It is very beautiful.

      B
From a distance.

      A
I wonder if it will survive?

      B
Ask Godot.

      A
He's gone.

      B
He's gone back down.

      A
Someone must be waiting for him.

      B
Do they have time?

ACT III

SCENE 2

Patients' Garden.

    DANIEL
I think you are God.

    GODOT
God, Godot – what does a name mean?

    DANIEL
I don't know. I suppose a name has associations.

    GODOT
And mine?

    DANIEL
Godot means one thing, God another.

    GODOT
Am I allowed to choose my own name?

    DANIEL
Sure.

    GODOT
I'll stick with Godot.

    DANIEL
Isn't God more appropriate?

GODOT
Why?

DANIEL
Look at what's happening to the world!

GODOT
What?

DANIEL
It's becoming sane!

GODOT
(Laughing)
You are so amusing.

DANIEL
I'm serious.

GODOT
Don't rob me of my enjoyment of you, Daniel. You are right, the world in fact is getting its act together, with a little help.

DANIEL
You mean you.

GODOT
I mean everyone here.

DANIEL
The world is conquered by crazies!

GODOT
No. The Inmates of the Hospital hold a mirror up to the inhabitants of the world so that they may see.

DANIEL
See what?

GODOT
Themselves.

DANIEL
Oh. And you?

GODOT
I do my bit.
(DANIEL smiles)

DANIEL
I'll never catch you.

GODOT
One day I'll catch you, and then you'll have me.

DANIEL
I'm looking forward to it.

GODOT
You must earn what you are given. Even I have not yet finished with that.

DANIEL
No?

GODOT
I have not earned you.

DANIEL
But you have.

GODOT
That's what you think.

DANIEL
You don't see it?

GODOT
(Puzzled)
No.

DANIEL
Look around.

GODOT
(Looks around)
I don't see.

DANIEL
No. You are only used to seeing pain, primarily your own. To you, life is pain. And the rest is – well, not there.

GODOT
Good Heavens!
(He feels renewed - happiness is coming to him. He smiles broadly, then laughs)
This is something!

DANIEL
From now on, this is everything.

GODOT
How did you do that?

DANIEL
We are all - all - being elevated.

GODOT
To what?

DANIEL
Bliss.

GODOT
Good Heavens! What about the badness?

DANIEL
A Presidential pardon.

GODOT
Future standards of behavior?

DANIEL
Godot is here – somewhere. He is supposed to keep us in line, anonymously.

GODOT
You mean we are all equal - with one exception? And he moves amongst us just like anyone else?

DANIEL
You got it?

GODOT
Aren't I clever?

DANIEL
What?

GODOT
This was the only way I could assure equality and still avoid disputes. I hope it works. I am a god just like any other, except that I act as a preventative, unrecognizable as such. I hope you don't mind.

DANIEL
No.

GODOT
I hope no one else minds either. It was all I could do to come up with this solution. Otherwise we would have had the broils of Olympus on our hands.

DANIEL
Yes. Look!

(Enter LADY DALY and BROWN on skates)

LADY DALY
Whew! Lancelot, you are a whiz!

BROWN
I am learning fast.

LADY DALY
If you don't, you'll break a few bones.

BROWN
And my head, too.

LADY DALY
Oh, forget your head. You broke that a long time ago. It's irreparable; when we have some time we can get you a new one.

BROWN
I like the one I have.

LADY DALY
So do most people, but I hear that isn't going to get them very far.

BROWN
What do you mean?

LADY DALY
Ask Godot.

GODOT
(To BROWN)
Have a problem?

BROWN
Not any more.

DANIEL
I hope they're all that easy.

GODOT
Onwards!

DANIEL
Upwards!
(Enter ALICE and LUCILLE OUTBACK)
Now that I am no longer aristocratic, I am not afraid of change.

LUCILLE OUTBACK
What about yourself?

ALICE
Least of all in myself. That is what I can influence most directly.

LUCILLE OUTBACK
I love you more and more, and I don't even live on Lesbos.

ALICE
We can move.

LUCILLE OUTBACK
Do you suppose the whole world will change?

GODOT
It has the opportunity to do so.

ALICE
But what if some parts don't?

GODOT
Then we leave them behind.

LUCILLE OUTBACK
Here.

GODOT
Perhaps. Does it matter? The Universe is a big place. The Earth is of very recent vintage. It can be disposed of. Not even its closest neighbor will take notice.

DANIEL
God.

GODOT
Yes?

DANIEL
You mean?

GODOT
The Universe is many billions of years old. You are practically the most recent arrivals. You are therefore the most easily dispensed with. Don't worry, the good shall be preserved.

LUCILLE OUTBACK
What about the rest?

GODOT
Do you really want to know?

DANIEL
No.

ALICE
Yes!

GODOT
The wicked will be reduced to nothing. That is all.

LUCILLE OUTBACK
Aren't you being a little hard on the wicked?

GODOT
It is they who are hard, not I. In any event, they will soon have had all the chances they need.

DANIEL
How many is that?

GODOT
An infinite number. Study Newton's infinitesimal. I don't think anyone on earth has yet mastered it.

DANIEL
I have.

GODOT
Good for you.

LUCILLE OUTBACK
I don't want to be wicked anymore. What do I do?

GODOT
Alice will help you, and Dottie, and Uncle Sturtevant, and whoever else is around.

LUCILLE OUTBACK
How do I avoid the crowds?

ALICE
Don't give them an opening. If you do and you get fleeced, save the evidence and call the police.

DANIEL
The police will be working overtime.

GODOT
They already are. There is time. For overtime.

DANIEL
Oh.

(Enter DOTTIE and UNCLE STURTEVANT)

DOTTIE DUMPLING
Darling.

UNCLE STURTEVANT
Don't put on airs. We have company.

LUCILLE OUTBACK
Whose house is this, anyway?

UNCLE STURTEVANT
We have taken it over. It was abandoned.

LUCILLE OUTBACK
Well it isn't now. We all live here.

UNCLE STURTEVANT
Oh. Well, I have papers.

GODOT
Burn them. Or yourself. Take your pick.
(UNCLE STURTEVANT burns paper)

GODOT
You know what you are doing?
(UNCLE STURTEVANT shakes head no)

GODOT
You are saving yourself. Any questions?

UNCLE STURTEVANT
Who are you?
(GODOT looks to sky)

DANIEL
Another applicant to screen. What caliber mesh do you use, Herr Professor?

GODOT
Whatever suits the applicant. There are many beyond saving.

DANIEL
There are many who don't want to be saved.

GODOT
Same thing. It is hard work, saving yourself. Not everyone is up to it.

DANIEL
But they all have their chance.

GODOT
Many chances, many.

DANIEL
Have you set a deadline? It might be wise, or we may be waiting indefinitely.

GODOT
Yes. Next Wednesday.

DANIEL
Let's see. Today is Saturday – five days if you count at both ends.

GODOT
I do. So did the Romans.

DANIEL
Yes. Five days. And we're close to the end of the first.

GODOT
Don't worry, I put them all on notice last night.

DANIEL
All?

GODOT
Everyone. The dream you dream and remember is the important dream.

DANIEL
Will they dream it again?

GODOT
No. Some people don't know how to use their intention.

DANIEL
Attention.

GODOT
Both.

DANIEL
How do we go?

GODOT
That is my secret - for the present. I don't want to create a panic, and I am not interested in last-minute conversions. I am not a member of the Catholic Church.

DANIEL
What are you?

GODOT
I am myself, just as anyone else. All the rest is words founded on fear.

DANIEL
Fear?

GODOT
It was one of the devil's inventions. Very clever, death. Preceded by ignorance. And then all the rest. You know.

DANIEL
Yes. I do.

GODOT
I have done what I can. Now I wait - with you.

DANIEL
I love you.

GODOT
Many people say that. Few do it.

DANIEL
They have a little time.

GODOT
A little. What would you like to do with yours?

DANIEL
Play chess?

GODOT
I am not good at games. Do you think anyone will care?

DANIEL
About their own salvation? Of course.

GODOT
The evidence so far is not in your favor.
(DANIEL is silent)

DANIEL
Is there anything we can do?

GODOT
Take the good ones with us -

DANIEL
And leave the rest behind. What becomes of them?

GODOT
I have friends elsewhere. They are prepared to bring my career to its conclusion.

DANIEL
You?

GODOT
My career, not me.

DANIEL
Then?

GODOT
Then, as I have said, we shall all be equals before eternity.

DANIEL
And the wicked?

GODOT
They will have been reduced to nothing: along with their wickedness.

DANIEL
I can't wait.

GODOT
We can't be too hasty. We don't want any potential angels to slip us by.

DANIEL
We must be impeccable.

GODOT
Yes.

DANIEL
All the time.

GODOT
Yes.

DANIEL
And everyone else, too.

GODOT
Yes. And if you make mistakes - make them impeccably.

DANIEL
Yes. Mistakes are not wicked unless the intention behind them is wicked.

GODOT
Daniel, A and B have done their job well.

DANIEL
And me?

GODOT
And you, too. Shall we have something to eat?

DANIEL
We have only water.

GODOT
That will do.

DANIEL
Oh. I thought -

GODOT
Food is for pleasure. The body is very nearly all water. It is like

a battery, a water-battery full of electricity. All it needs most of the time is water.

DANIEL
I am not a biochemist.

GODOT
Neither am I.

DANIEL
Well, what would you like to do with your time?

GODOT
Make love.

DANIEL
But that is not allowed.

GODOT
By whom?

DANIEL
The Authorities.

GODOT
Who are they?

DANIEL
I don't know.

GODOT
Let us ignore them. They are of no account.

DANIEL
But they may kill you.

GODOT
They already have. Many times. And I am still here.

DANIEL
You are.

GODOT

The problem with previous inmates is that they allowed themselves to be killed. Catholicism is founded on cannibalism made into a cult. And the starting point is a murder. Can you imagine wearing a cross for life? It is lugubrious.

DANIEL

How did it get started?

GODOT

Don't ask me.

DANIEL

I won't. If we're not having dinner, what are we doing?

GODOT

Listening to the flowers.

DANIEL

Listening to the flowers? I thought one -

GODOT

Shh. Listen:

(He recites)

    I'd never seen them there before,
    It was as though the flowers were at war,
    The lungwort and the hellebore.
    But at closer sight,
    It was my mind that had put
    Each flower to flight,
    In fact, theirs was a dance
    Celebrating the marriage of a prince
    of Elms to a common maiden of the moss,
    A match that adumbrated no loss
    Of love on either side,
    Lacking impediment of pride,
    For love was the true metal
    That sent every petal

On its flight along the ground:
Love makes a sound
That even the deaf can hear,
So don't close up your ear,
The flowers are speaking to you very near.
I write in my spare time.

DANIEL
Oh, Mr. Godot, your poem is a treasure, and so are you.

GODOT
That's my job. Being a treasure.

DANIEL
Who gave it to you?

GODOT
I volunteered.

DANIEL
Volunteered?

GODOT
No one else wanted it.

DANIEL
Good Heavens!

GODOT
That's not what I would say. But it was my choice.

DANIEL
Couldn't you, well, tell what would happen?

GODOT
I suppose, but if I did, that would take all the air out of my tire. What would be the point? Unitary Omniscience? Perfect Protoplasm? I would rather be here with you, the flowers, my poem and -

DANIEL
A few clouds overhead.

GODOT
Soon enough they will go, and so will we.

DANIEL
What about the other Inmates?

GODOT
They are making the right choices. They have suffered enough, and so have we. Do you have faith in me?

DANIEL
Yes, yes.

GODOT
It is so hard to know sometimes, people do such strange and terrible things.

DANIEL
The devil -

GODOT
Yes, yes, the devil. He only provided the opportunity - the rest made their choices.

DANIEL
Why not continue -

GODOT
I am tired of the pain, and I think everyone else is, too. For those who aren't -

DANIEL
"The rest is silence."

GODOT
You got it.

DANIEL
Who wrote that?
(GODOT points to himself)

DANIEL
One more secret revealed.
(He laughs)
Where else have you been, my friend.

A
(To DANIEL)
You look very handsome.

DANIEL
It must be the weather.

GODOT
(To A)
Or you.

A
(To GODOT)
Or you.

GODOT
Soon enough we shall all have the powers of Proteus.

DOTTIE DUMPLING
Do you believe that?

UNCLE STURTEVANT
I think I need a few miracles to convince me.

GODOT
Back to the Catholics, eh? You need something to prop you up?

UNCLE STURTEVANT
Faith is a tricky thing.

DANIEL
Either you have it or you don't. Faith founded on miracles is not faith.

GODOT
Would you like a miracle?
(UNCLE STURTEVANT nods yes. GODOT nods and UNCLE STURTEVANT disappears in smoke)

DOTTIE DUMPLING
Where is he?

GODOT
He has been reduced to nothing.

DOTTIE DUMPLING
I don't believe you.
(She starts to cry)

GODOT
(About to nod again)
This is going to be a busy day.

DANIEL
Stop! Bring him back!

GODOT
Why? I am sure nothing is an improvement over this.
(He looks around)

DOTTIE DUMPLING
(Very sad)
He liked flowers. And your poem.

GODOT
Oh, well.
(UNCLE STURTEVANT reappears with some smoke and lightning)

UNCLE STURTEVANT
Why do you look like that?

GODOT
Miracles have that effect on some people.

UNCLE STURTEVANT
I don't believe in them.

GODOT
(To DOTTIE DUMPLING)
Here's your chance.
(DOTTIE DUMPLING is silent)

GODOT
Another time - I guess you don't love me as much now. And yet I shall bear full responsibility for what happens at the end.

DANIEL
Full responsibility?

GODOT
Yes, Daniel. It is part of who I am. I have already made my choices.

DANIEL
Can't you change?

GODOT
I can only go forwards, not backwards. The only way to go backwards is to start all over again, and that is something I definitely choose not to do. Things are arranged that way for you, too.

DANIEL
So we are all, everywhere, well acquainted with Hell.

GODOT
Yes.

DANIEL
And babies?

GODOT
Raw recruits, full of potential. I do not believe in Original Sin. Babies are not ready to make choices. When they begin, then their scales begin to weigh their souls.

DOTTIE DUMPLING
As it were.

GODOT
As it were.

UNCLE STURTEVANT
Am I sick again or are we being set up again for a fall?

GODOT
Neither. You are alive. Consider life the opportunity to improve yourself.

DOTTIE DUMPLING
In every way. See, Darling?

UNCLE STURTEVANT
Yes, yes, I see. But I like myself the way I am.

GODOT
Most people do. Otherwise they could not live with themselves. Now, why are you here?

UNCLE STURTEVANT
Because I could not live with myself.

GODOT
Now, do you want to change?

DANIEL
Oh, Uncle -

UNCLE STURTEVANT
Yes, I do. I do want to change. From my feet to my head. Ahh! There is so much to do!

GODOT
Daniel will help you. And Dottie, too.
(All three go to another part of the garden)

A
Monsieur Godot?

GODOT
Oui?

A
Now that we have finished waiting -

GODOT
But you haven't.

B
What!!

GODOT
The story is not over.

A
What's left?

GODOT
You want me to give it all away, FREE? The resu;ts would be dreadful, or, well, non-existent. I want something for me money, so you two wait - you'll get to the end with the rest of us.

A
Well, are we all going to die?

GODOT
Oh, well. You all are dead. That is why you are here. If you had been reduced to nothing, you would not be here. You would not be anywhere.

A
We're ghosts?

GODOT
That's about it.

A
And this is –

GODOT
Heaven – or part of it. The earth and heaven have amalgamated.

A
Where are the little devils?

B
Don't ask too many difficult questions.

GODOT
It's alright. The little devils were reduced to nothing.

B
When?

A
While we were talking. There must be a mess to clean up.

GODOT
There is always something for everyone to do.

B
Something for everyone.

A
I like that.

B
I think I love life - death, even ours.

A
Oh, B, now we are free! It didn't even hurt.

    B
I was not aware of it.

    GODOT
No. Only I.

    A
Thank you.

    B
Thank you.

    GODOT
You have yourselves to thank. You made the right choices.

    B
But you gave us choice.

    GODOT
Yes. Well. What else could I do? Create a puppet theater in which all the characters were mine?

    A
I don't think that would teach you much.

    B
We have learnt a lot from observation.

    GODOT
So have I.

    A
But –

    GODOT
What about the pain? As I have already said, I am a curious person, and I needed more knowledge than most.

    LADY DALY
Now Lancelot –

BROWN
Yes, my love.

LADY DALY
I feel different today. What's in those pills you give me?

BROWN
Nothing. They're placebos. Always were.

LADY DALY
What?

BROWN
Placebos. Sugar pills. Nothing. Though I do hear that some of your doctors prescribed poison for you.

LADY DALY
I'm dead.

BROWN
What!? You took them??

LADY DALY
Of course. So I must be dead.

GODOT
In Heaven we are all dead.

BROWN
We're in heaven?

LADY DALY
Looks that way. Here, you do the laundry today. I'm gonna go get a degree in psychology.

GODOT
Excuse me. Lady Daly - you already know more than most psychologists. Furthermore, they are now out of power, or should I say out of business.

LADY DALY
What can I do?

GODOT
Enjoy the flowers –

A
And the birds –

B
And the trees and ferns.

BROWN
And honeybees.

GODOT
Nature has much to teach us –

BROWN
Nature has much for us to enjoy.

GODOT
Find it, listen to it, it sings of all that is good in the world, even death, for death is always making room for rebirth and renewal.

LUCILLE OUTBACK
So I'm dead. Prove it.

ALICE
Shall I shoot you?

LUCILLE OUTBACK
Hah!

(ALICE pulls out a gun and shoots LUCILLE OUTBACK, who staggers a bit and then recovers her equilibrium)

LUCILLE OUTBACK
Missed!

ALICE
Right on target.

LUCILLE OUTBACK
My chest has a hole in it. You're right. Even if I wasn't dead, I am now. But what about you, Alice? Are you with me?

ALICE
I took an overdose last night. I'm deader than a duck.

LUCILLE OUTBACK
Trite but true. And the rest?

ALICE
They're all with us?

LUCILLE OUTBACK
Even Brown?

ALICE
Yes.

LUCILLE OUTBACK
He should change his name again.

ALICE
I suggest you keep your comments to yourself. Or you may end up downstairs.
(LUCILLE OUTBACK looks alarmed)

LUCILLE OUTBACK
Now that we are dead, what do we do with ourselves? Drink?

ALICE
That is one way to kill time.

LUCILLE OUTBACK
That is one way to kill yourself.

ALICE
It's slow, but it works.

LUCILLE OUTBACK
Great way to fool yourself into thinking you still are alive.

ALICE
Yes. How are you doing? Now that I'm dead, I don't find alcohol necessary or attractive. It tastes terrible.

LUCILLE OUTBACK
Yes. I've given it up.

ALICE
What about all those parties?

LUCILLE OUTBACK
Pure emptiness.

ALICE
You are not empty.

LUCILLE OUTBACK
Nor you.

ALICE
Do you like it here?

LUCILLE OUTBACK
Yes.

ALICE
Shall we stay?

LUCILLE OUTBACK
Let's.

ALICE
Any application to fill out?

LUCILLE OUTBACK
No one's thrown us out.

ALICE
True.

LUCILLE OUTBACK
Let's stay.

ALICE
Yes.

BROWN
I cannot bloody understand it. Every time I prick your finger, I get no blood.

LADY DALY
We have already had our bloodletting. And there is no more blood left.

BROWN
But you need blood to be alive.

LADY DALY
The obvious conclusion -

BROWN
(Screams)
You're dead!

LADY DALY
(Laughs)
Hey, honey, don't get too agitated or you'll need a placebo to calm you down. Anyway, I hate the sight of blood, especially my own. It makes me faint.

(Suddenly there is a bright light shining on a spot on stage. GODOT walks into the spot and disappears)

LUCILLE OUTBACK
Where's he gone?

DANIEL
To find a few fresh souls to translate up here.

LADY DALY
Up here?
(Stage is engulfed in clouds)

DOTTIE DUMPLING
Looks like we really are on high.

LADY DALY
Or high on high.

DANIEL
Just high.
(The clouds consume everyone)

-FINIS-

www.ingramcontent.com/pod-product-compliance
Lightning Source LLC
Chambersburg PA
CBHW030156100526
44592CB00005B/299